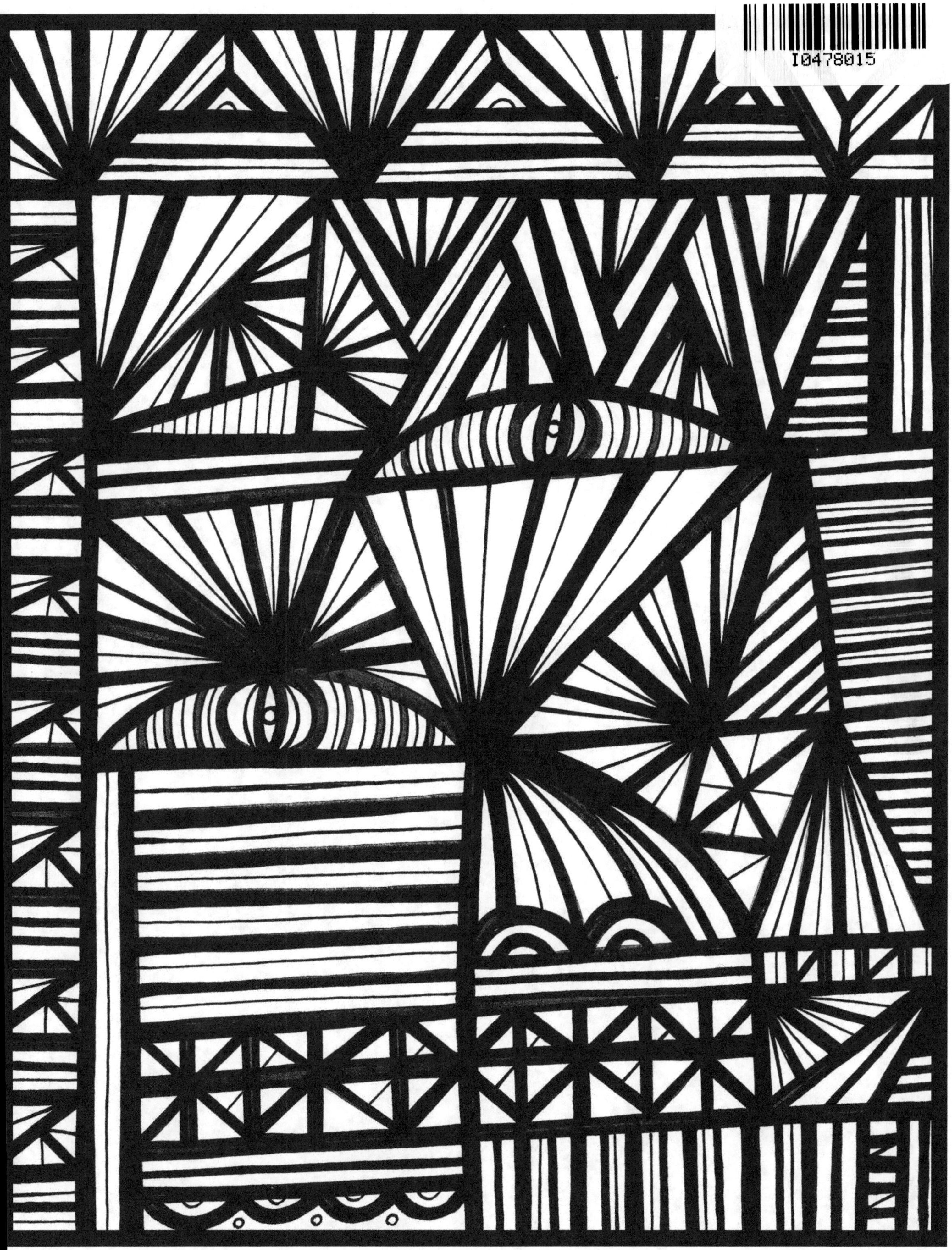

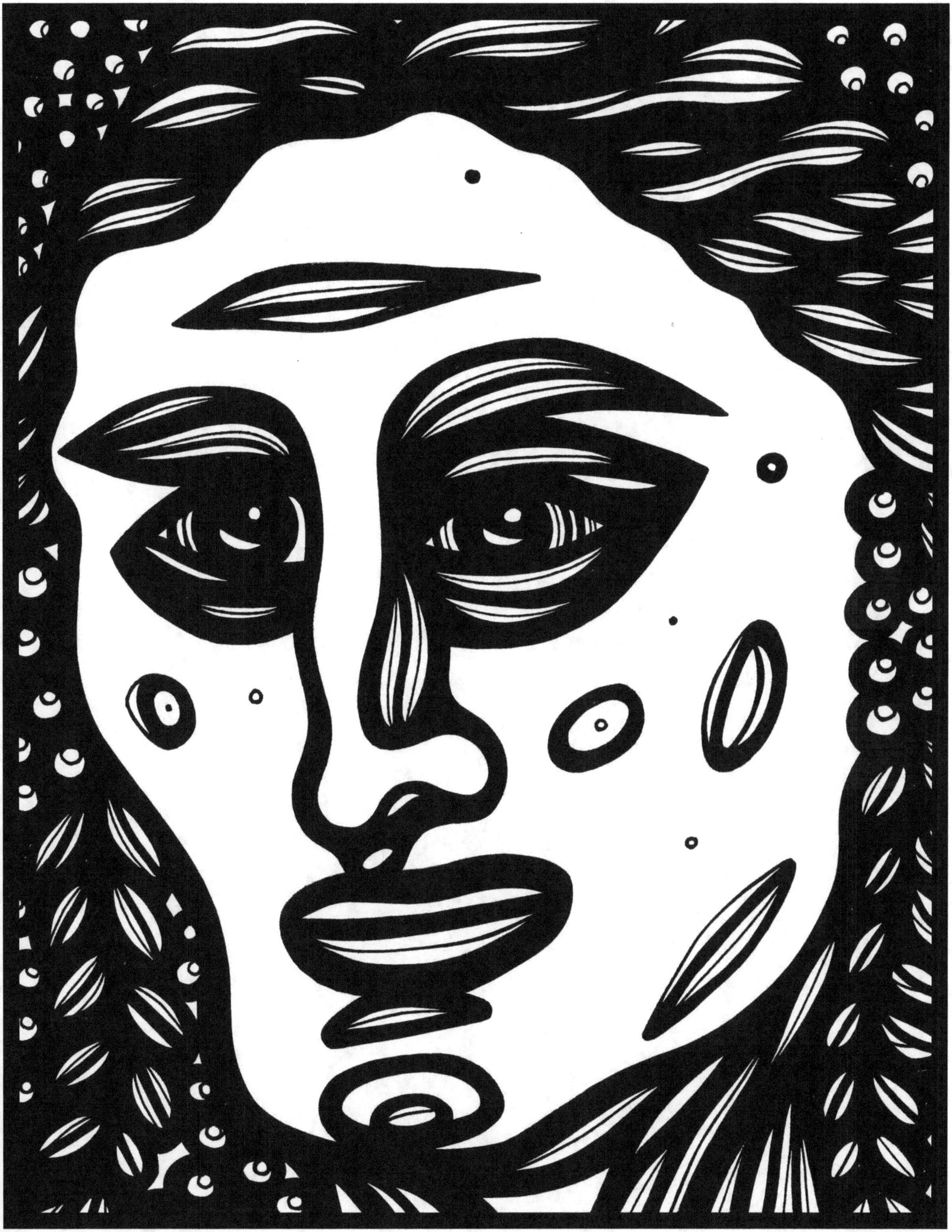

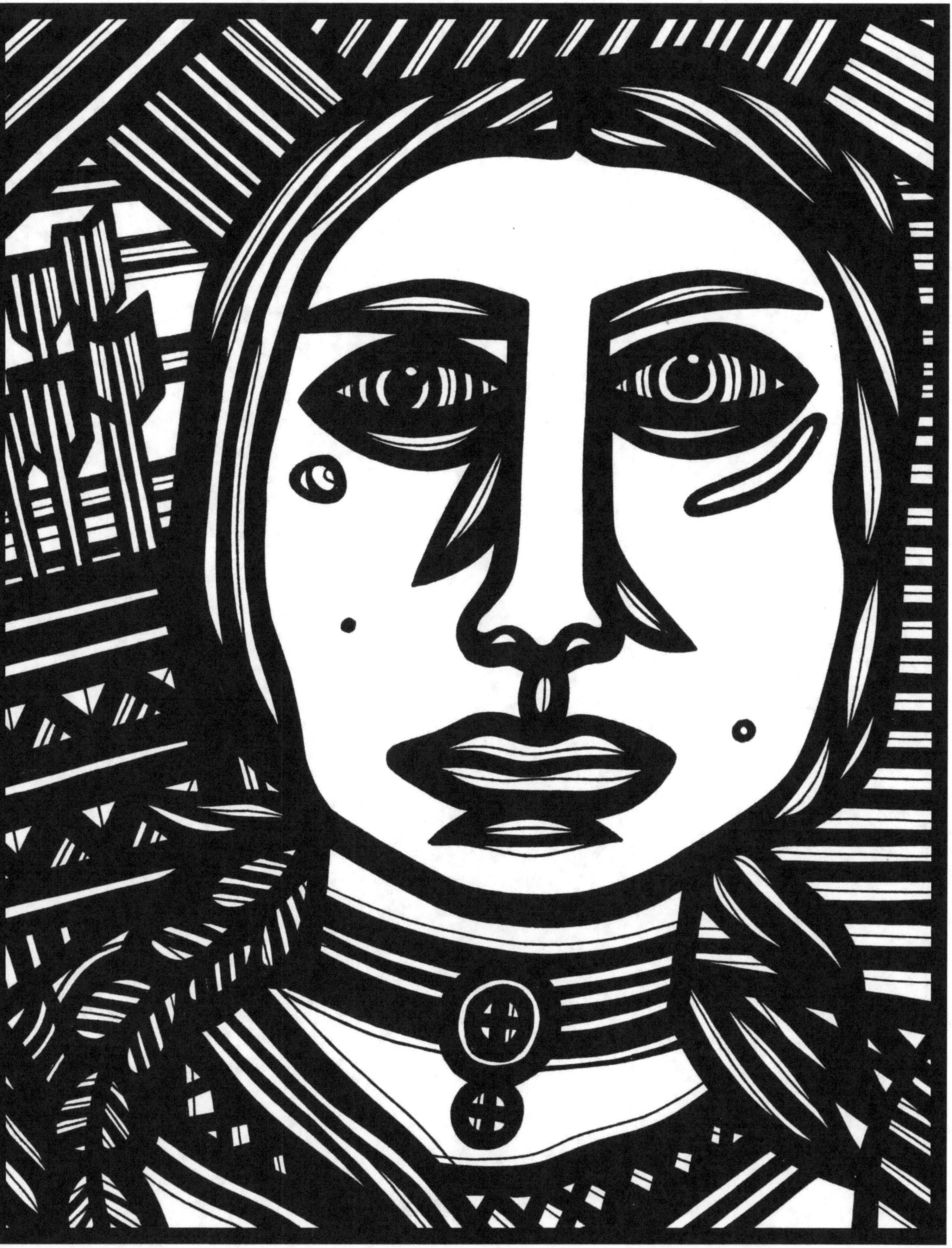

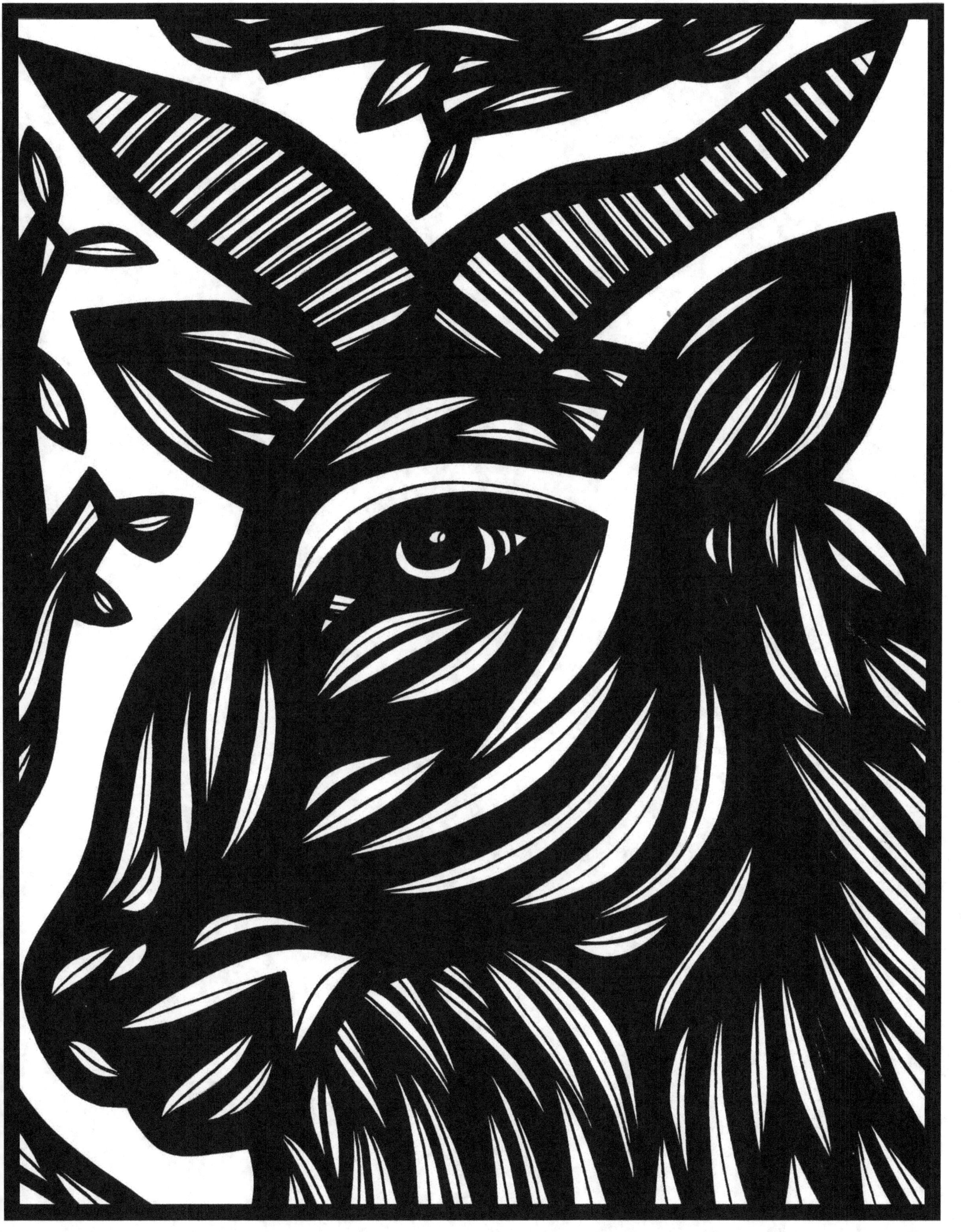

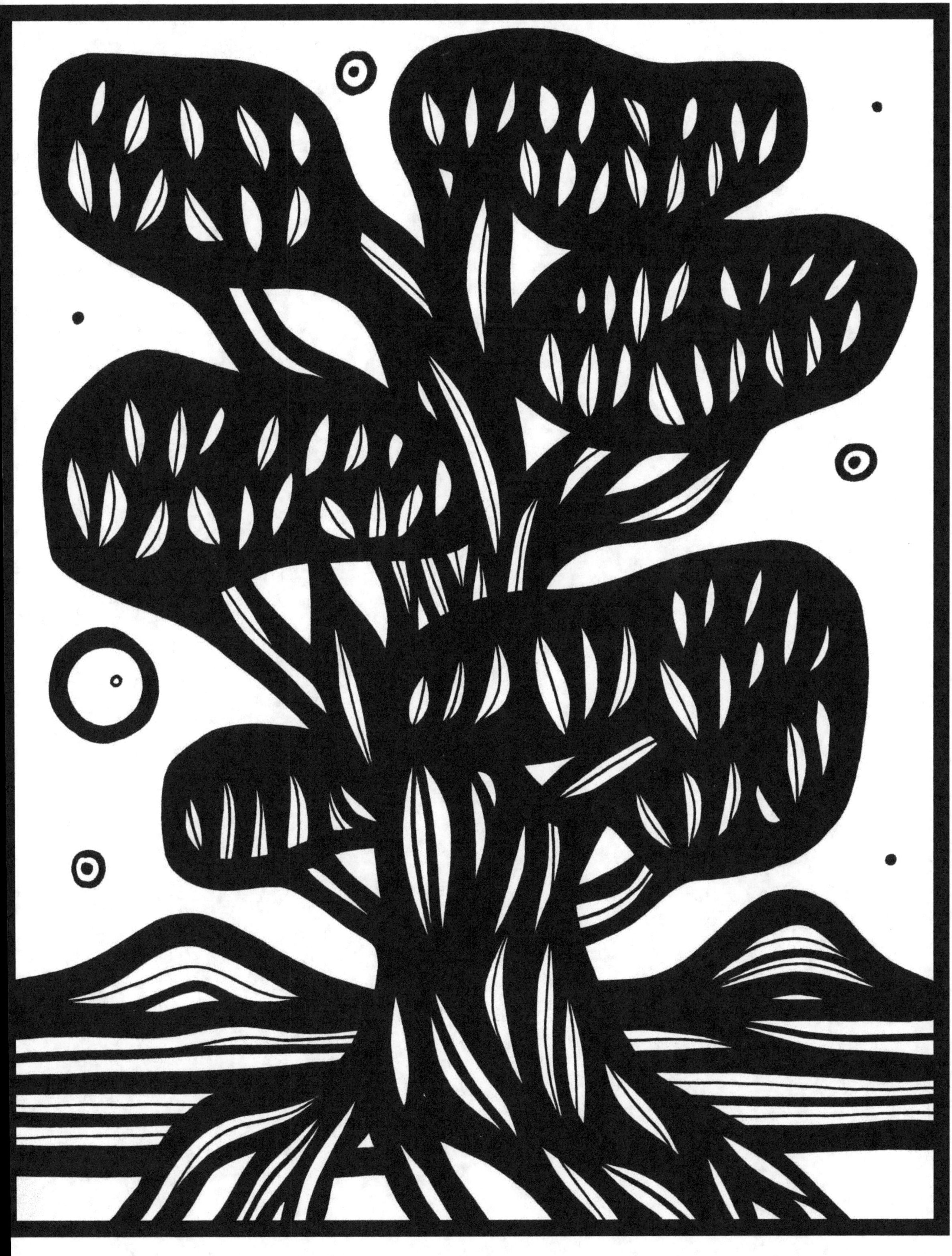

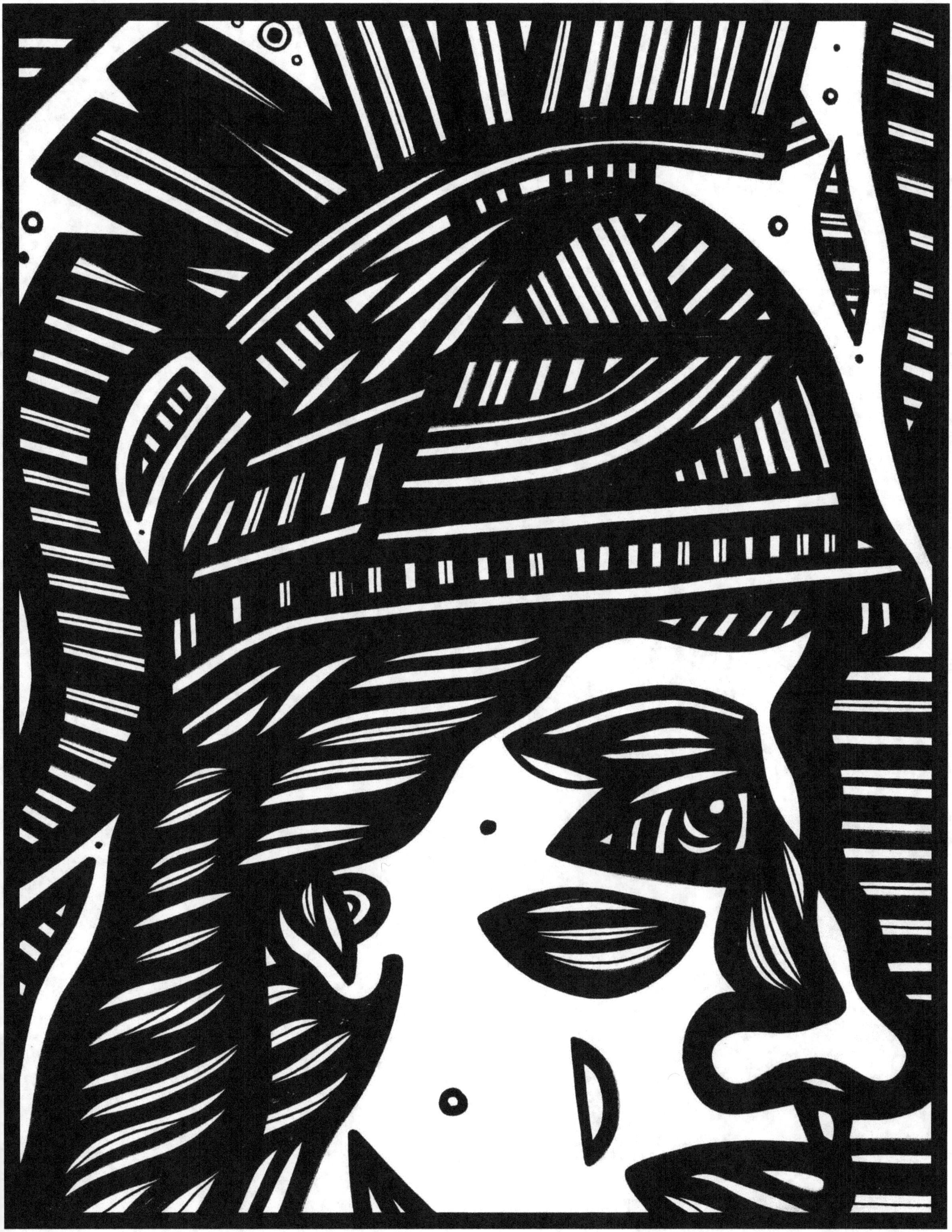

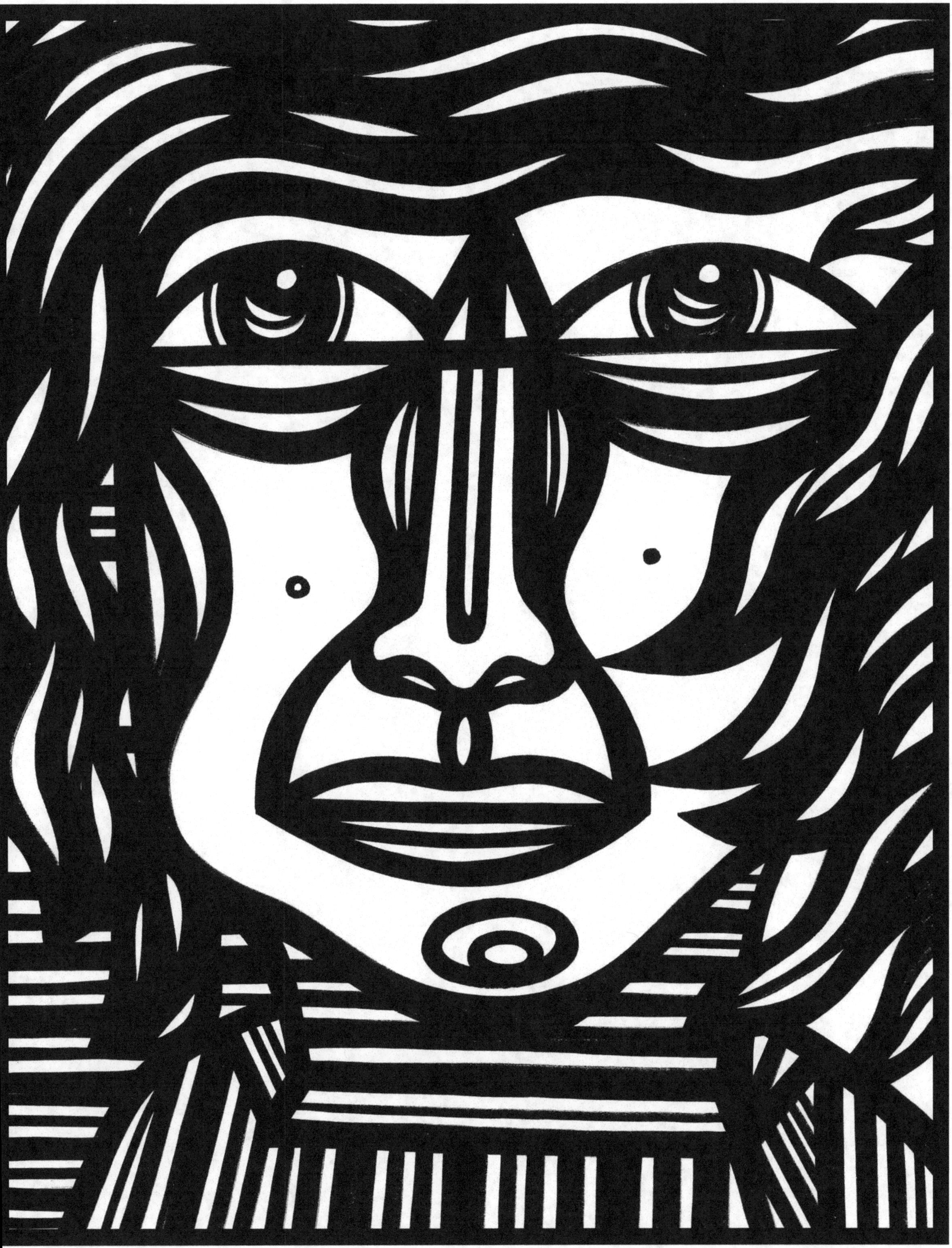

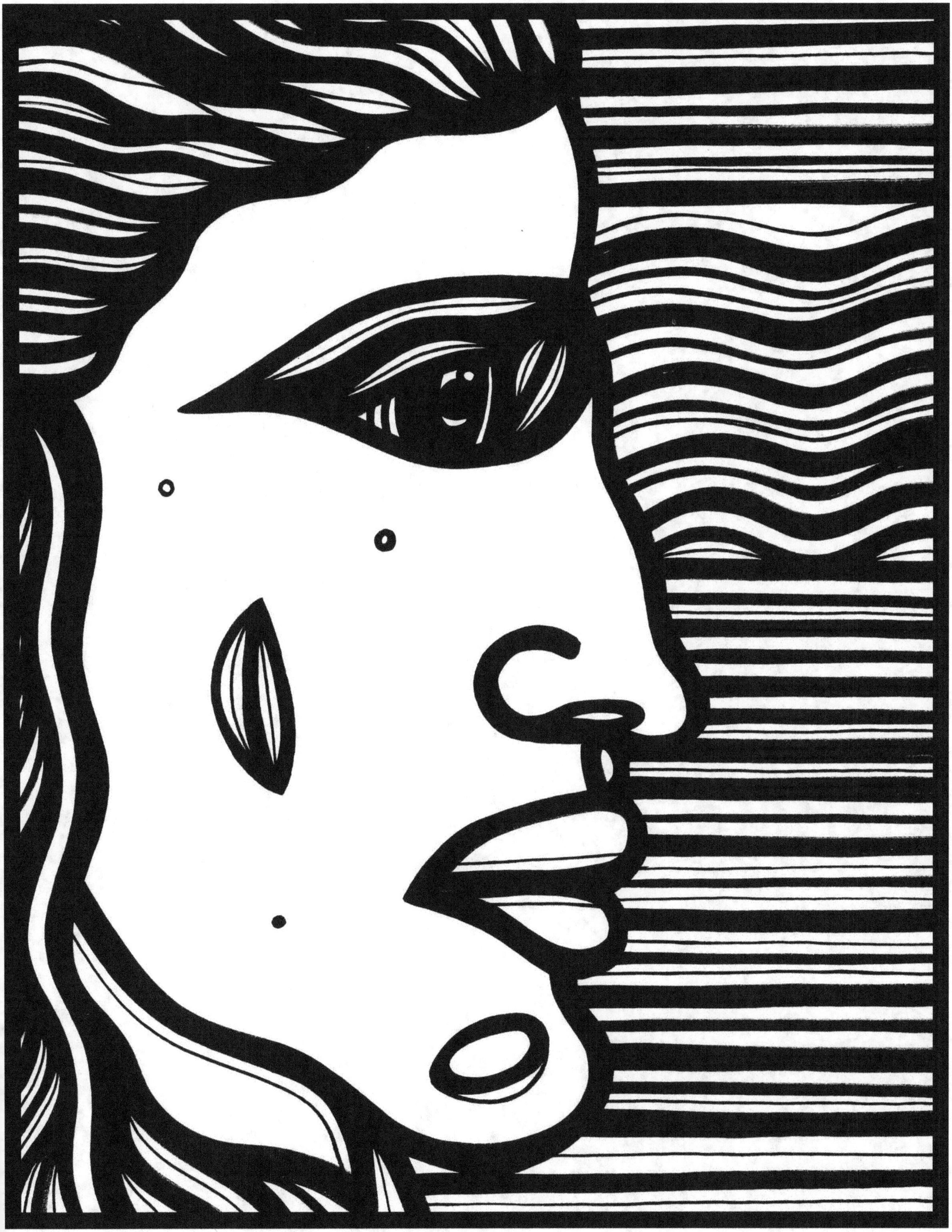

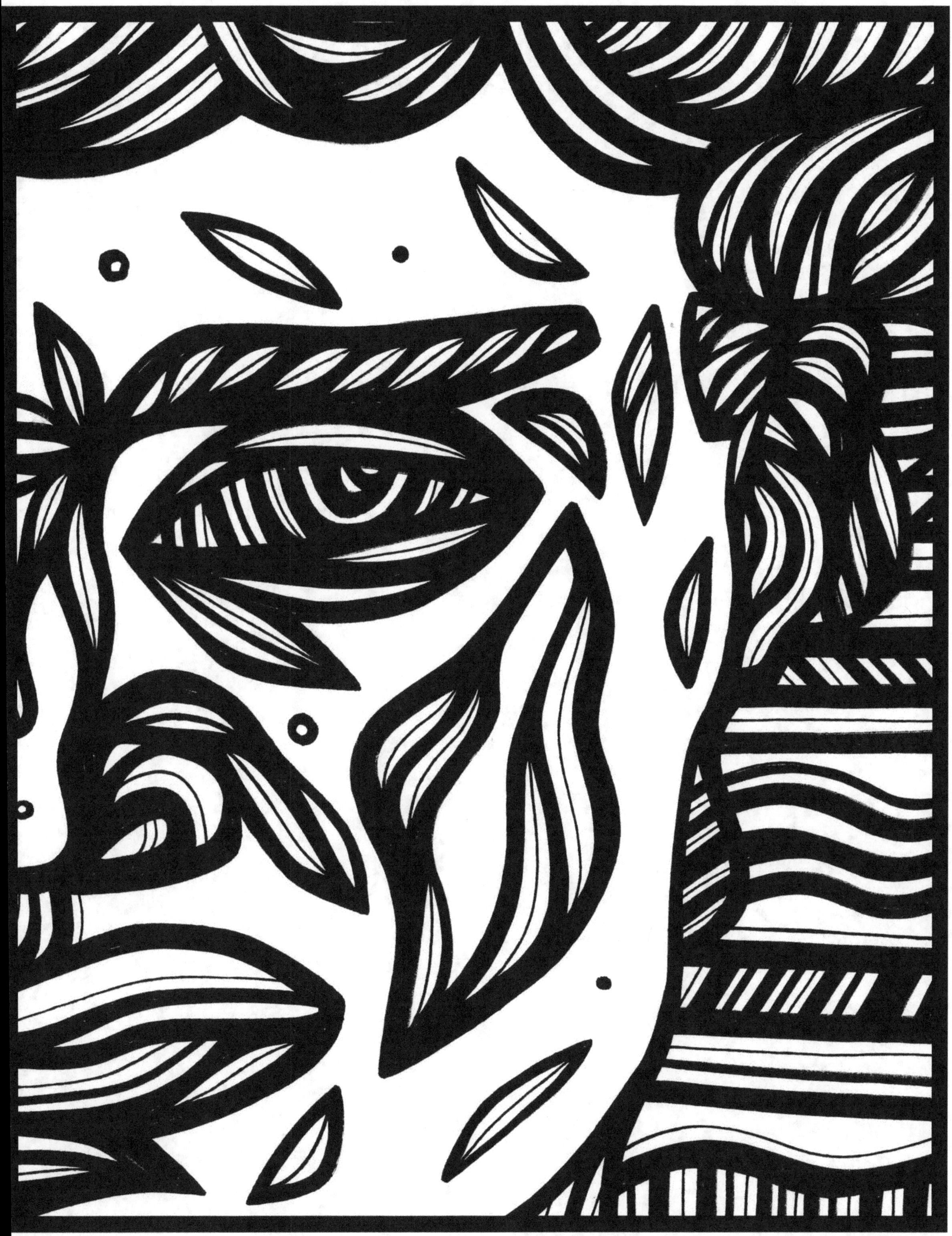

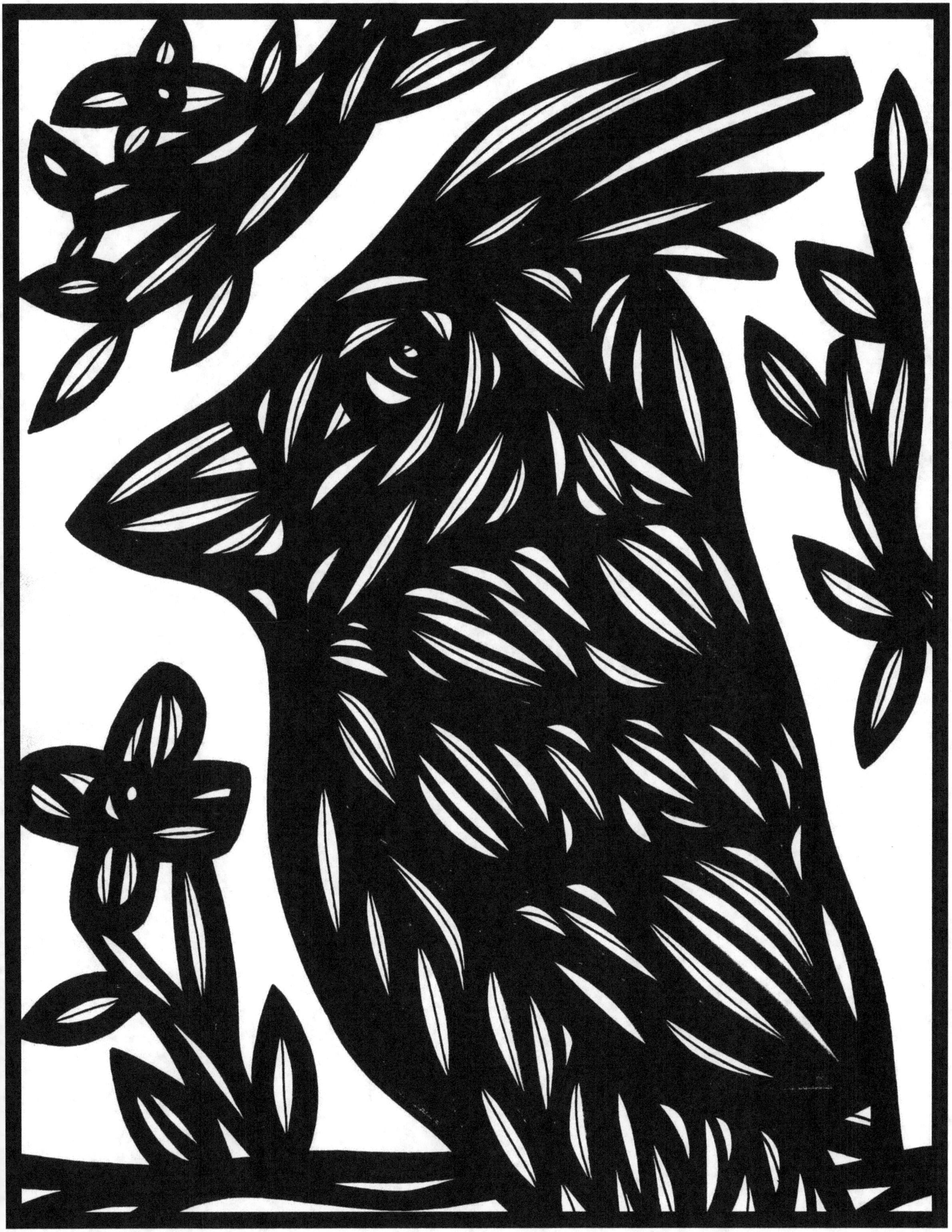

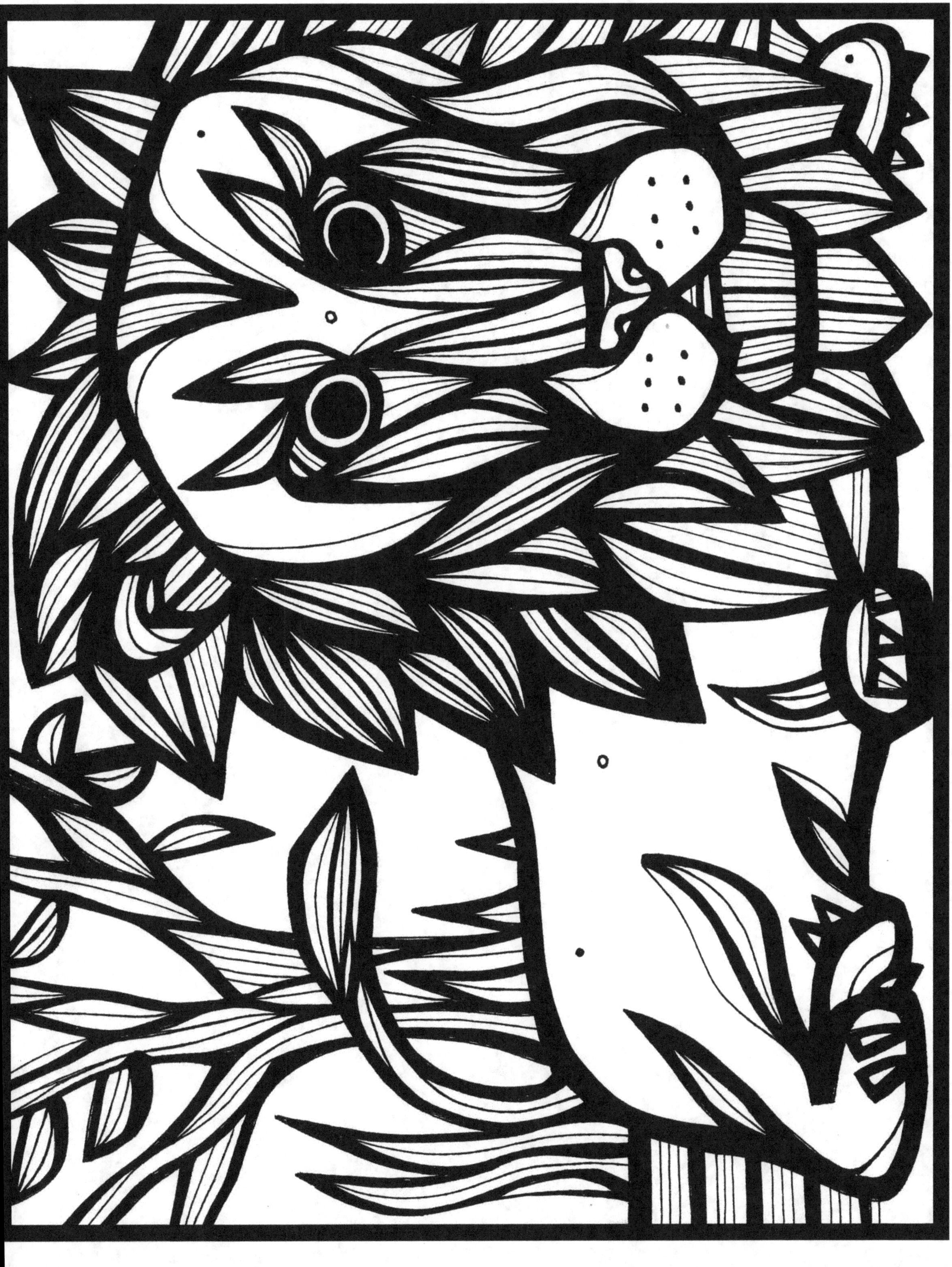

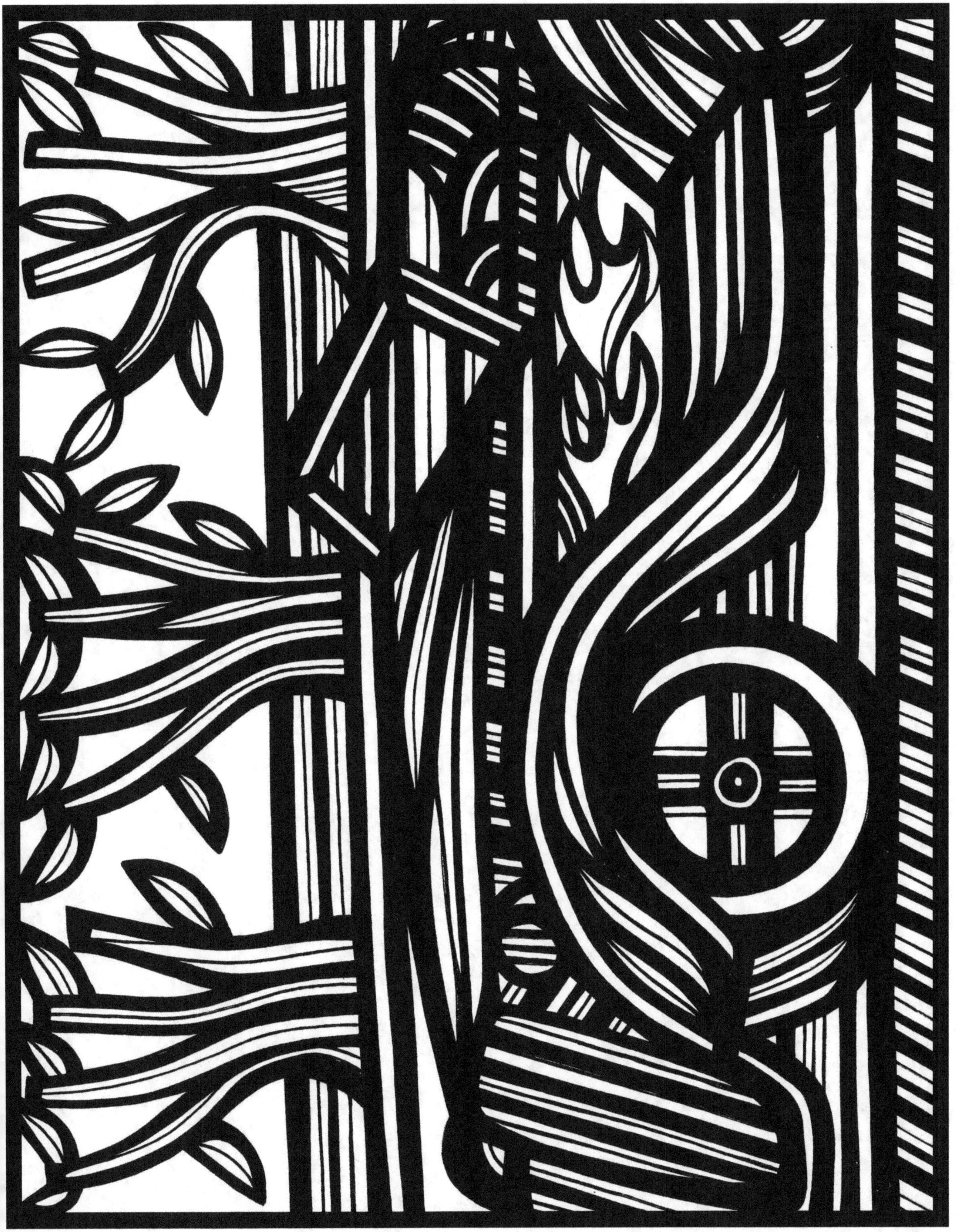

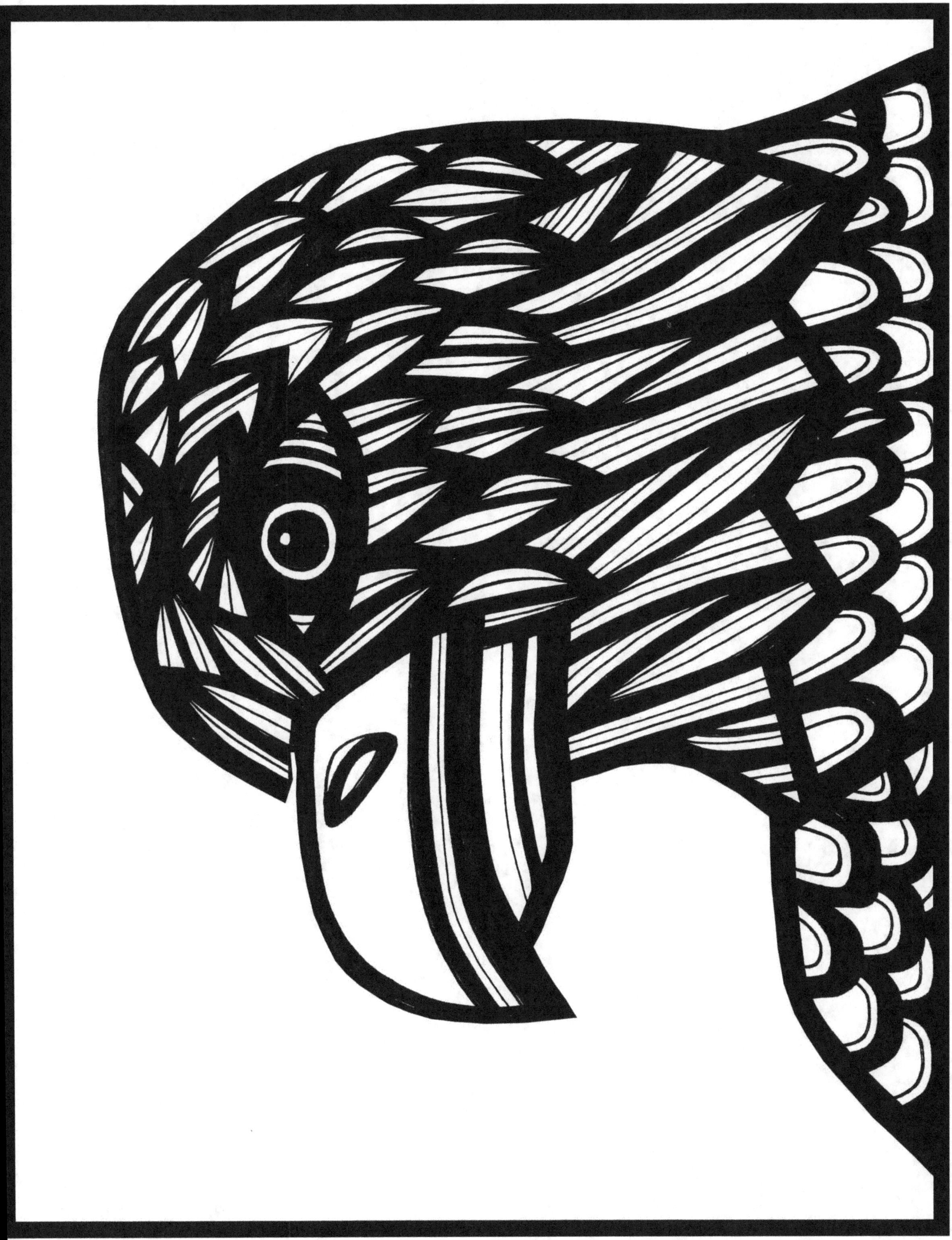

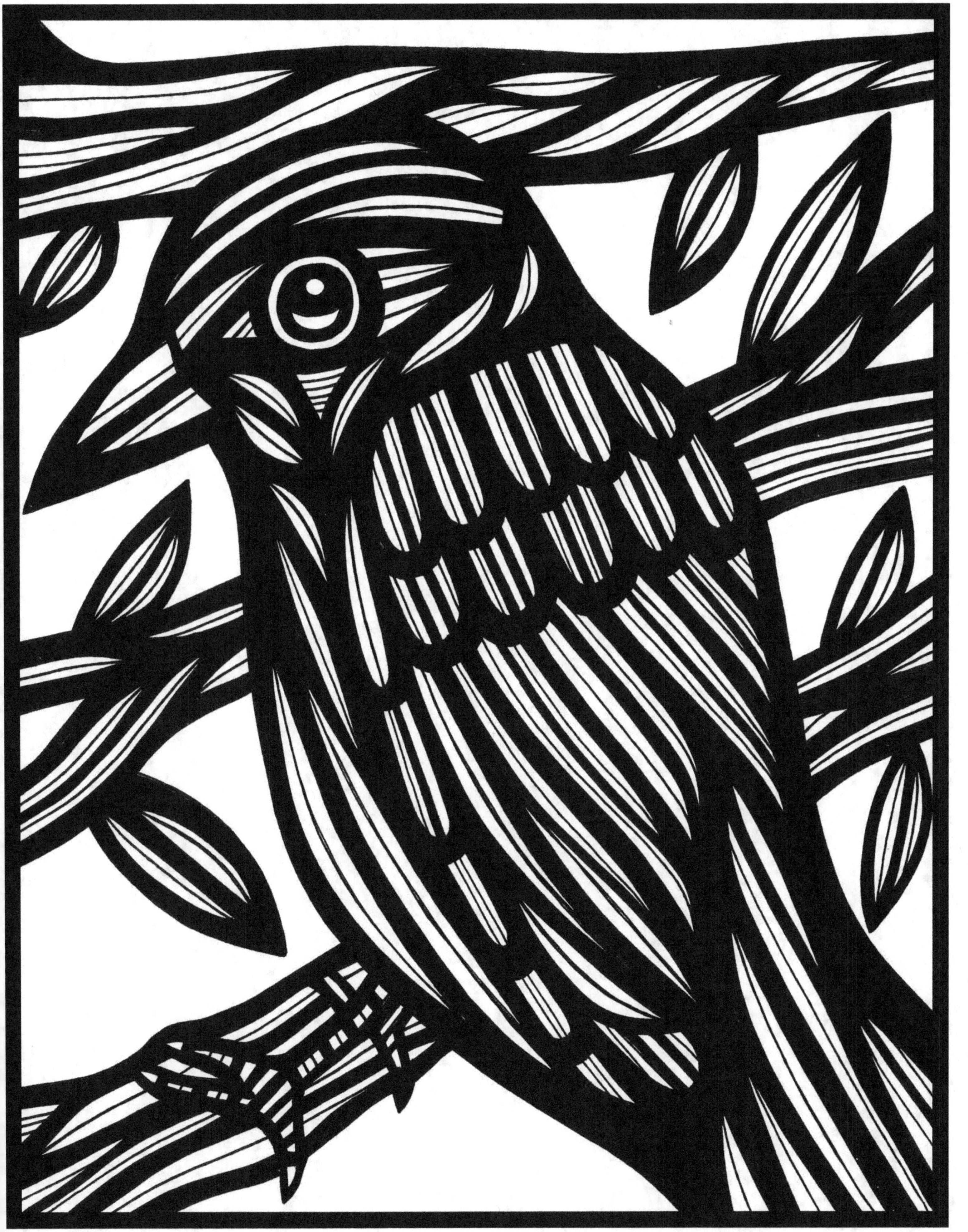

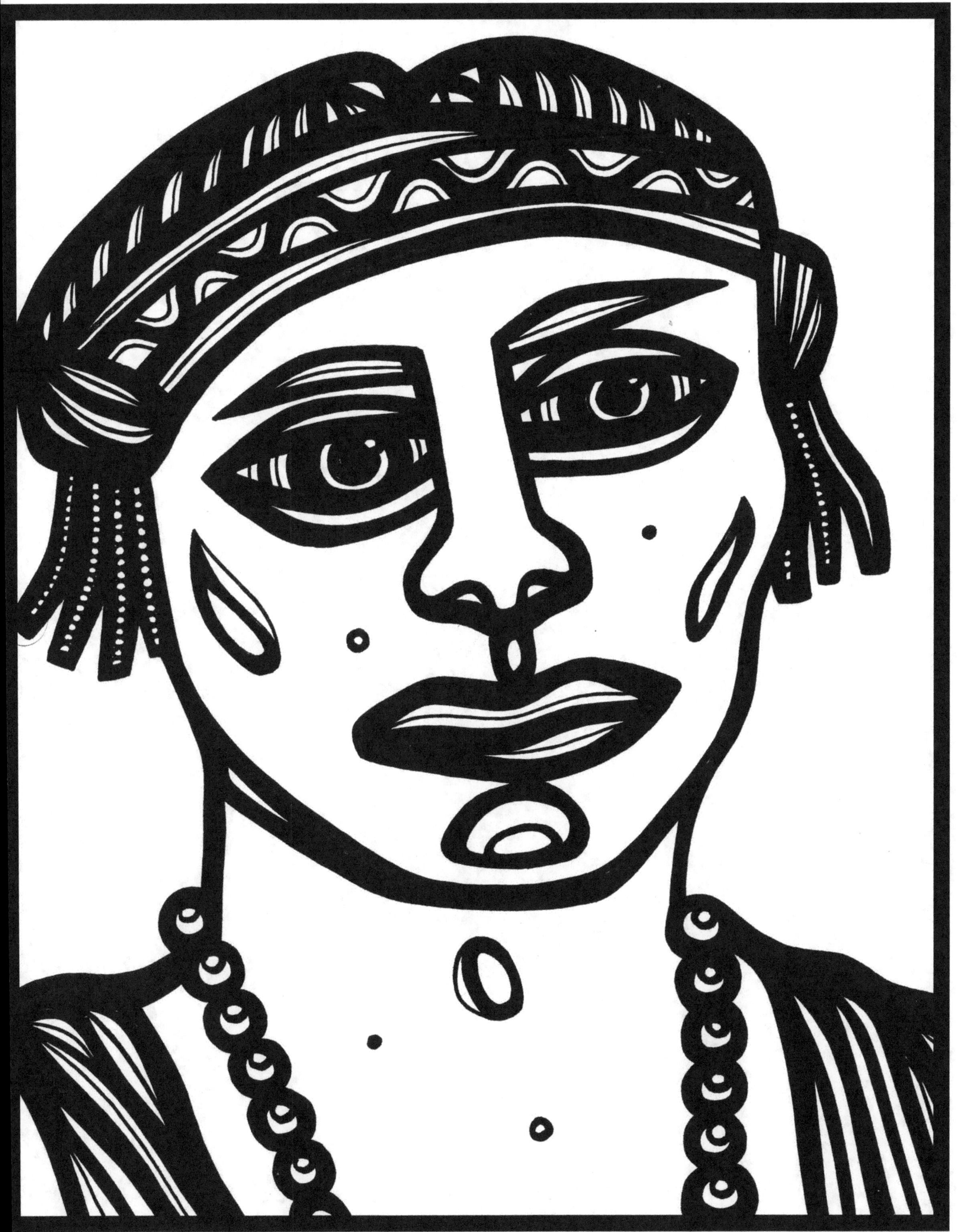

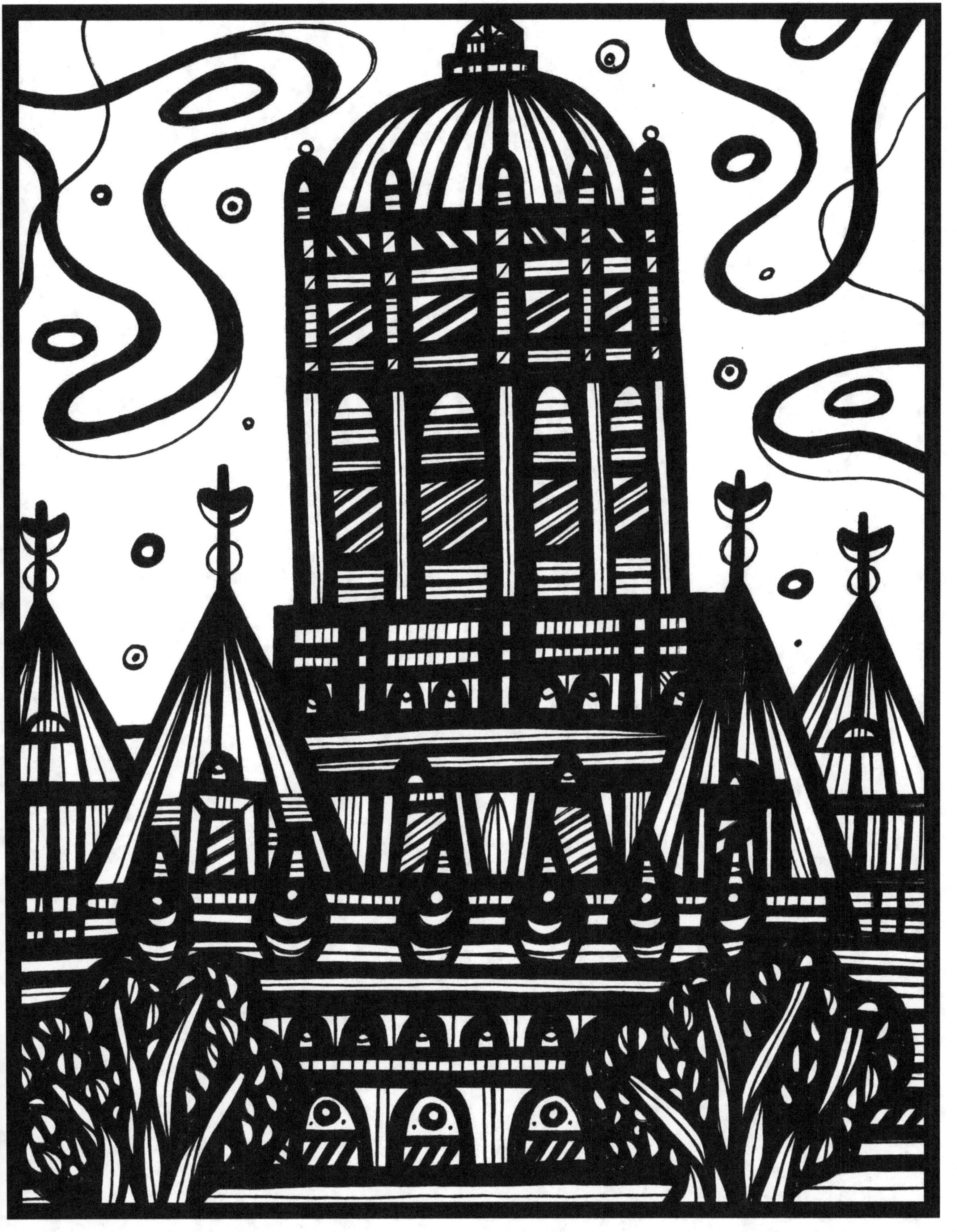

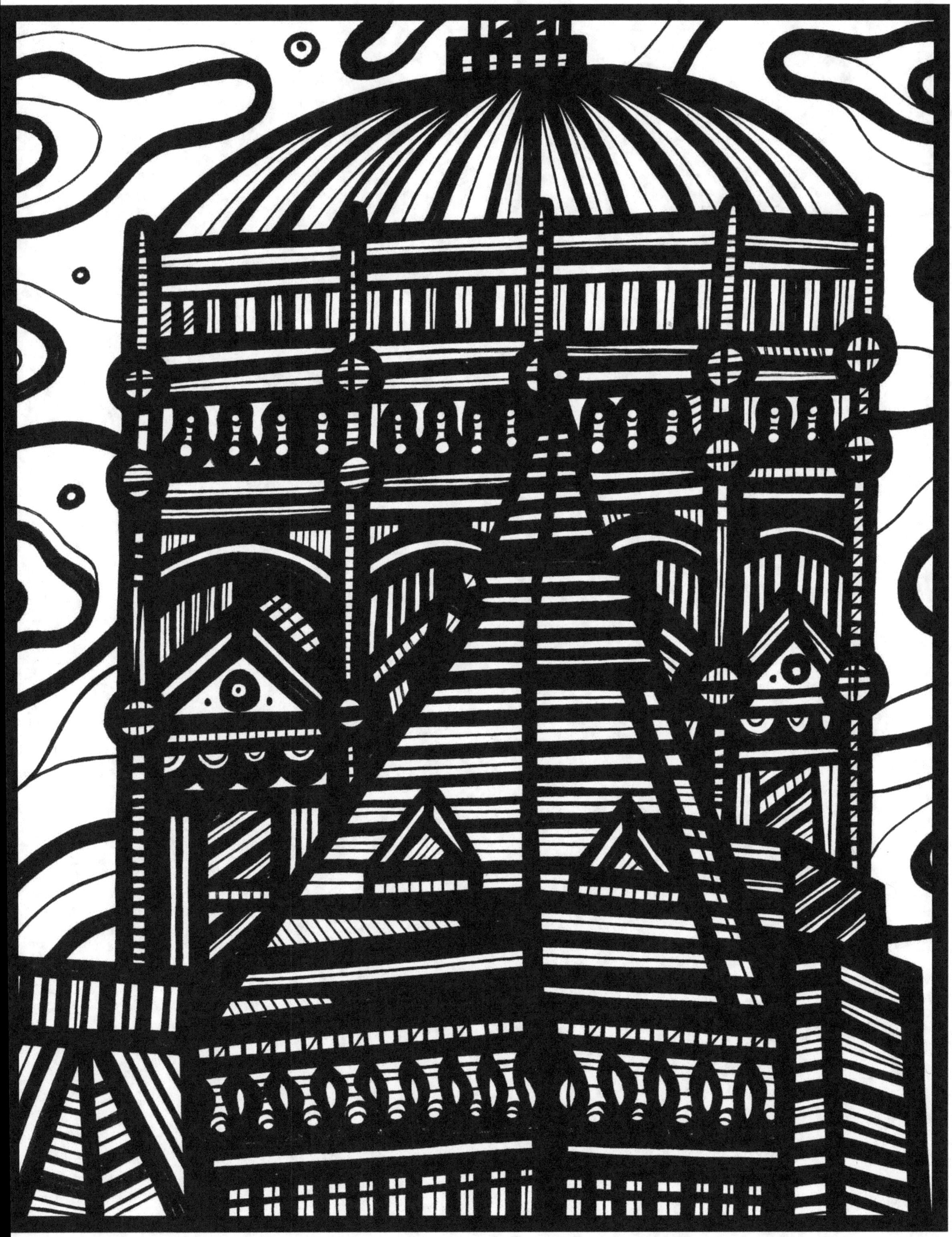

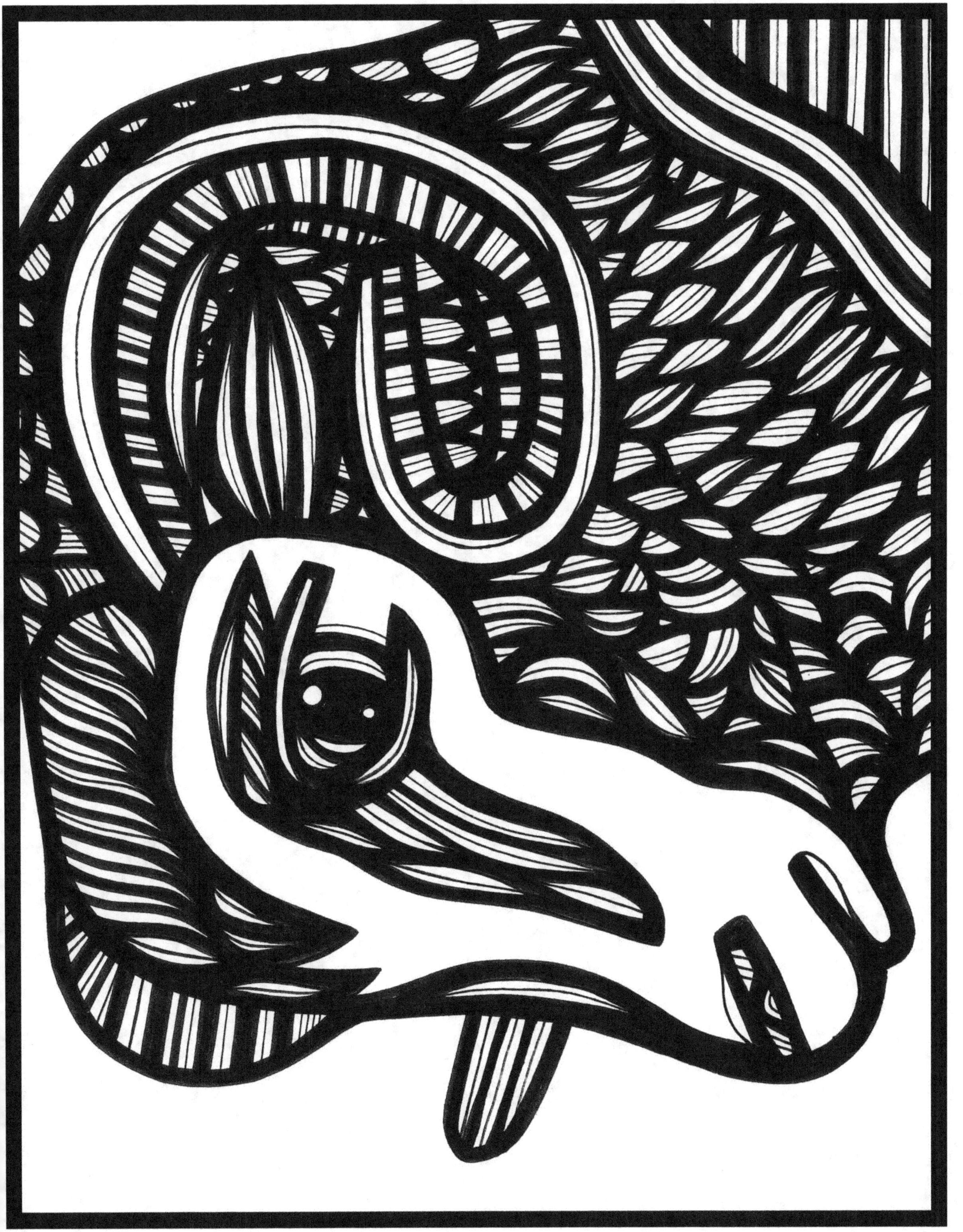

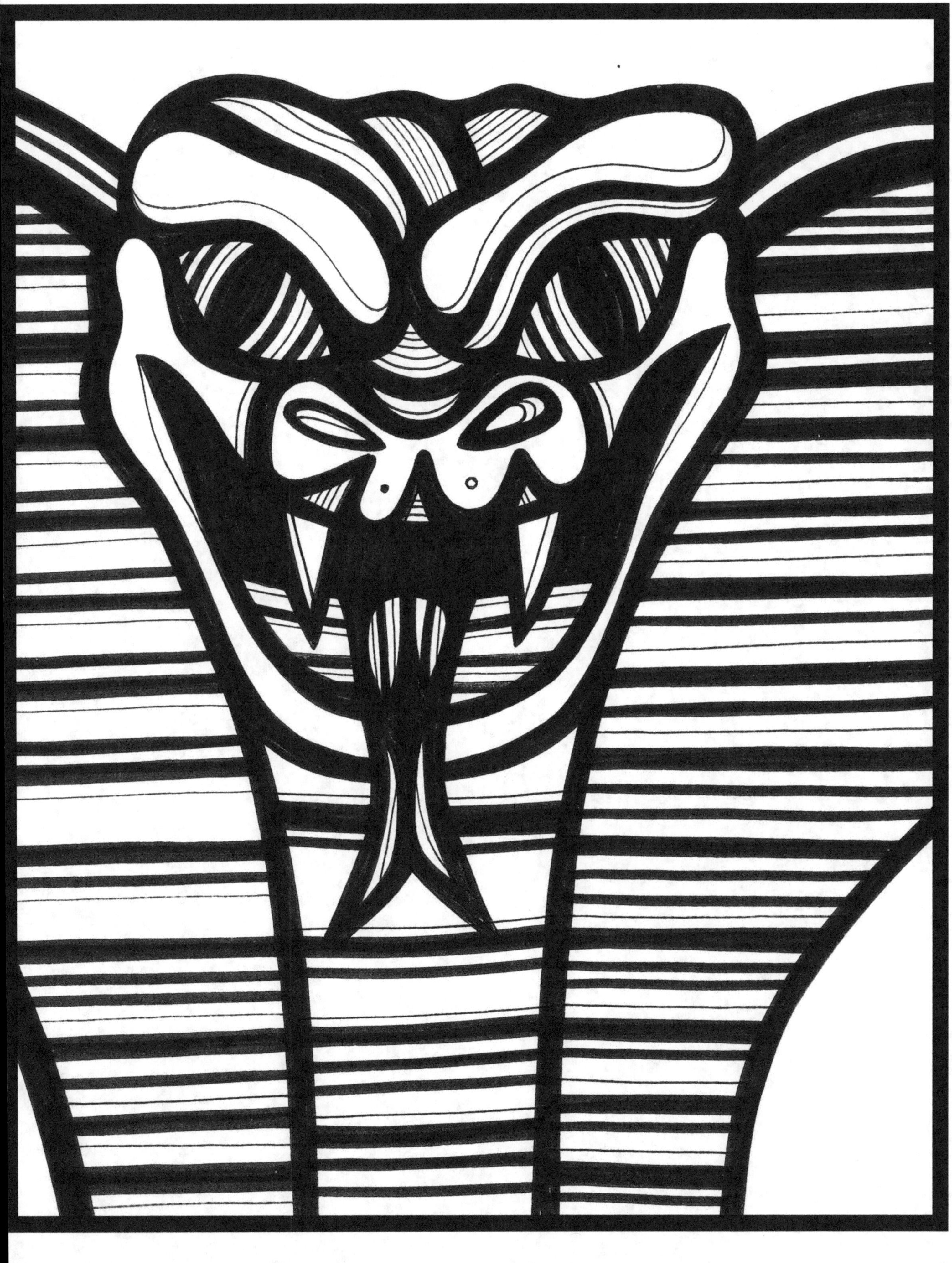

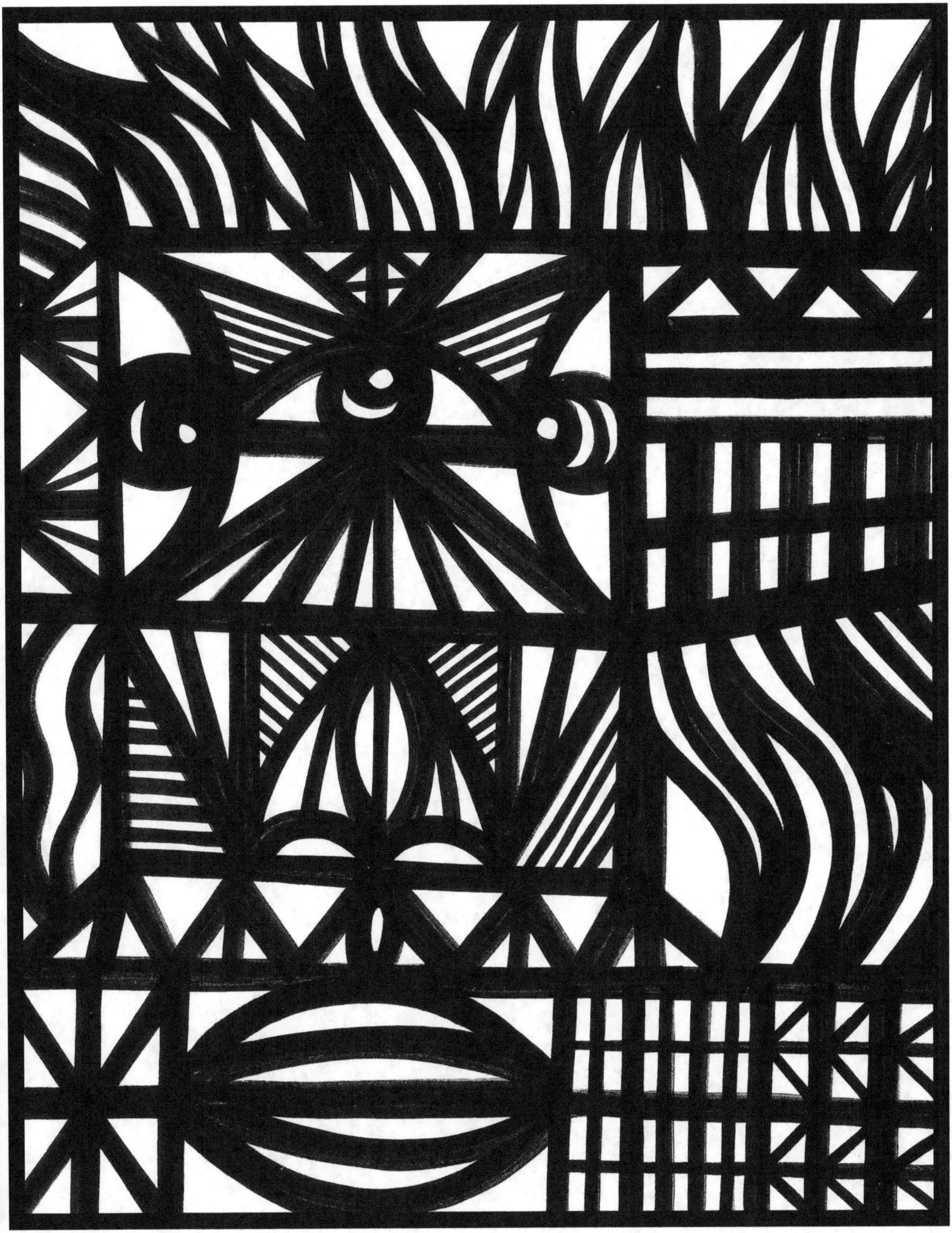

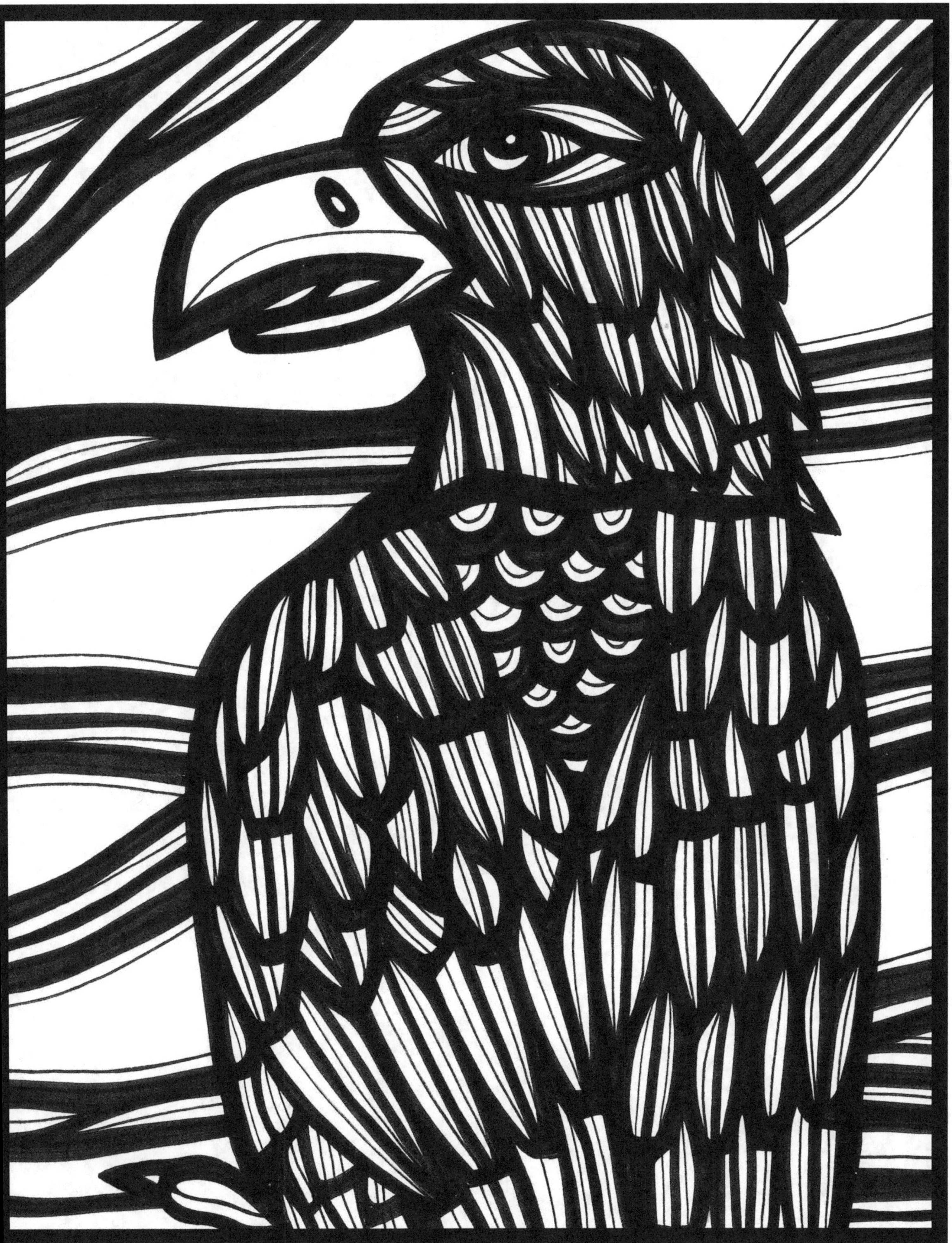

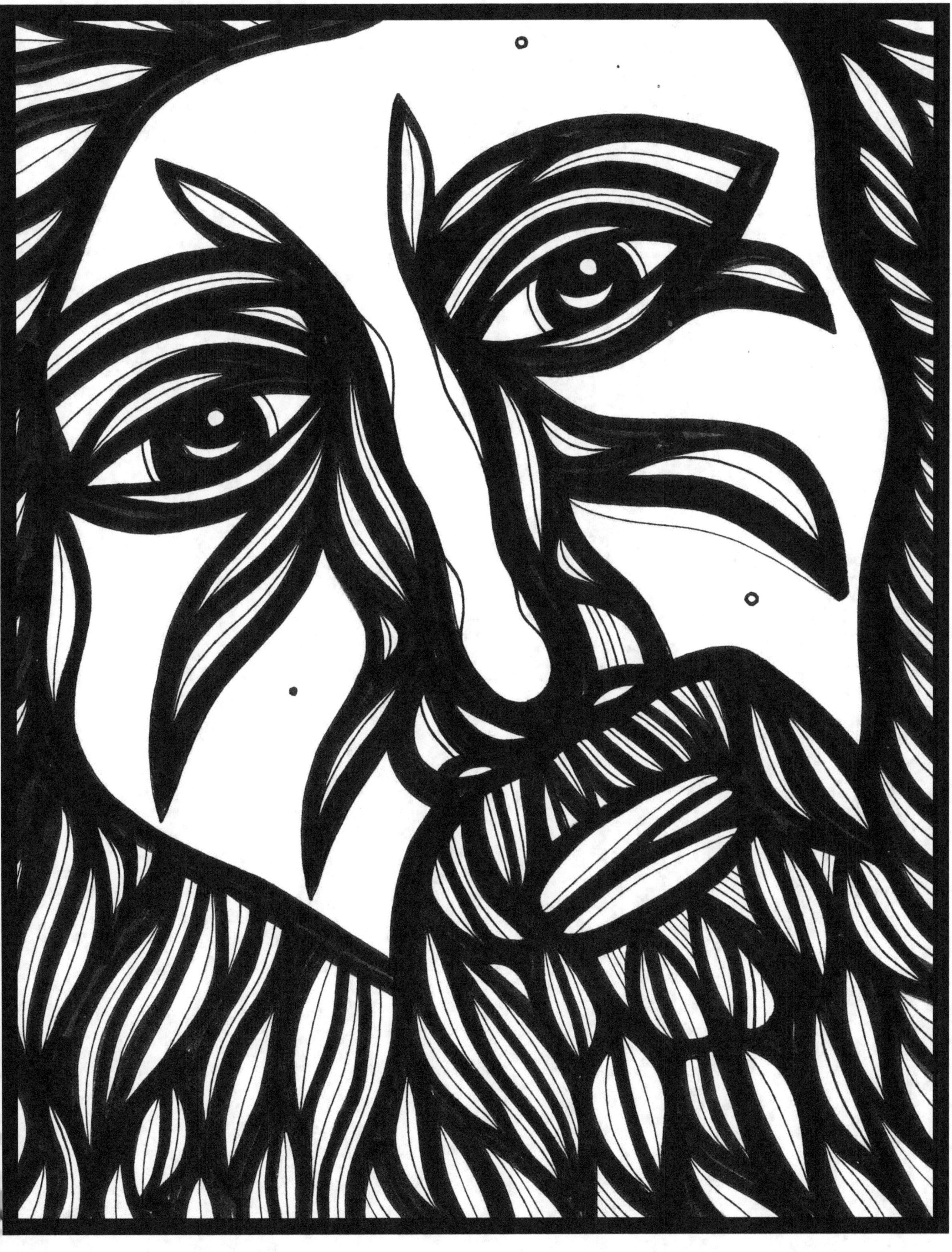

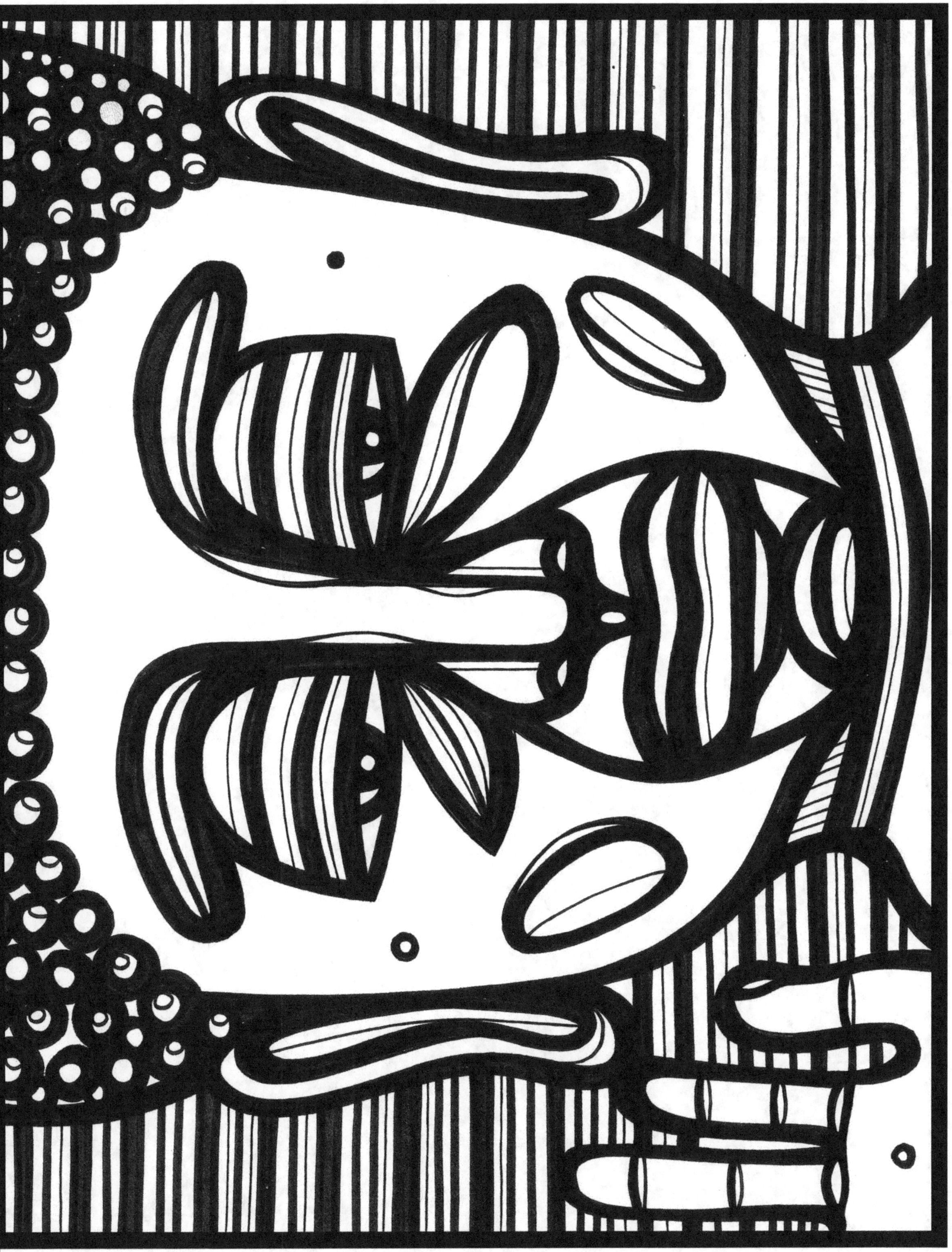

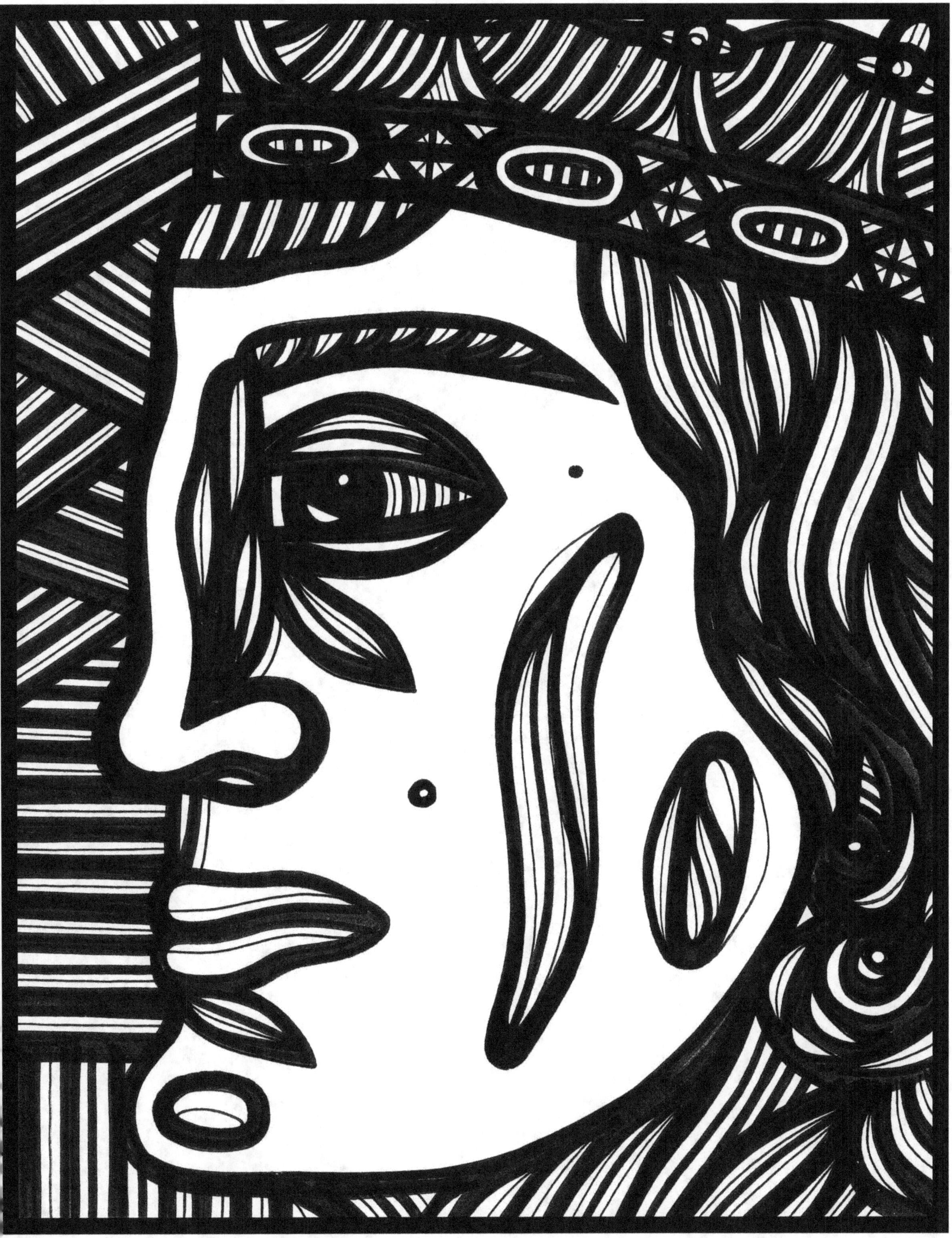

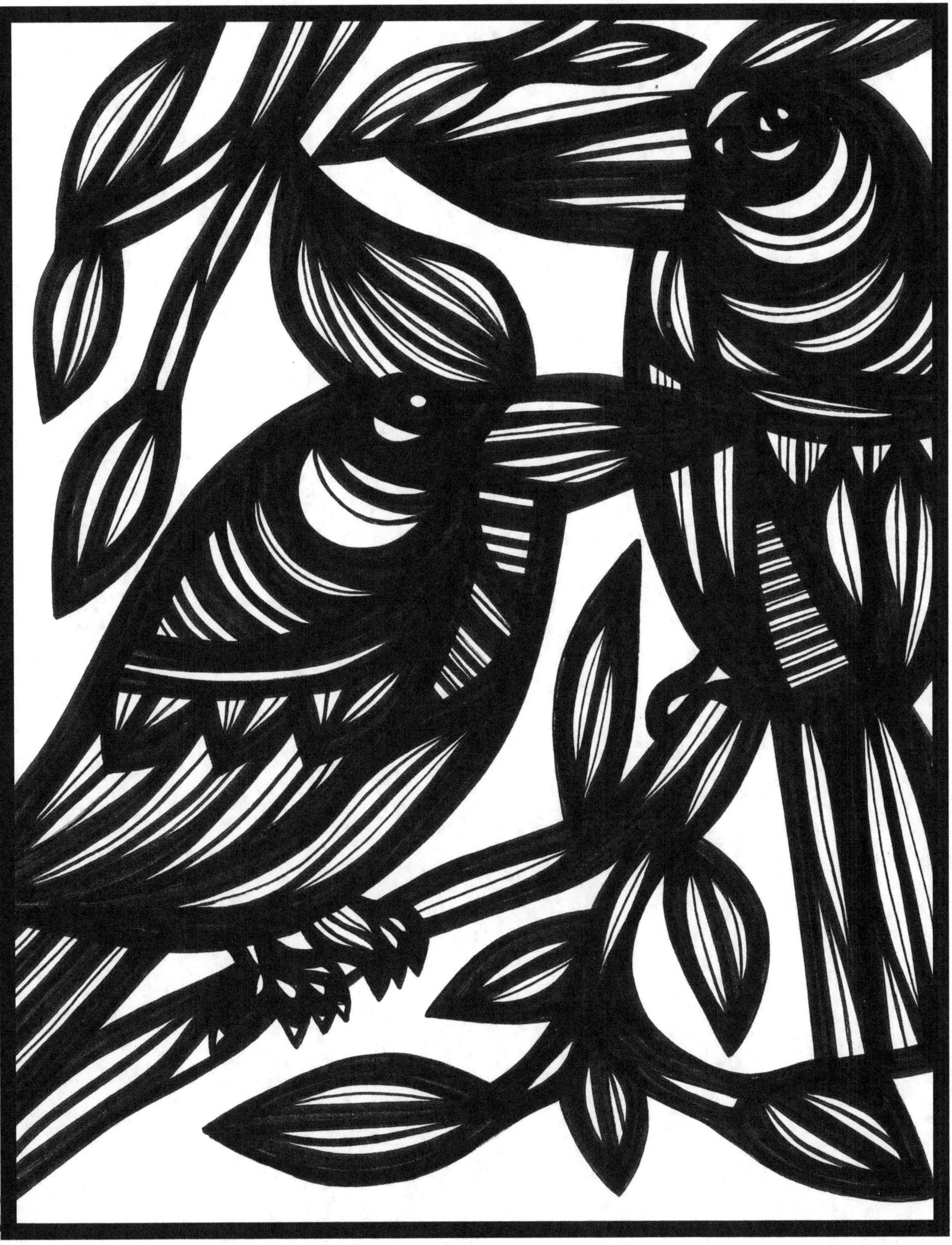

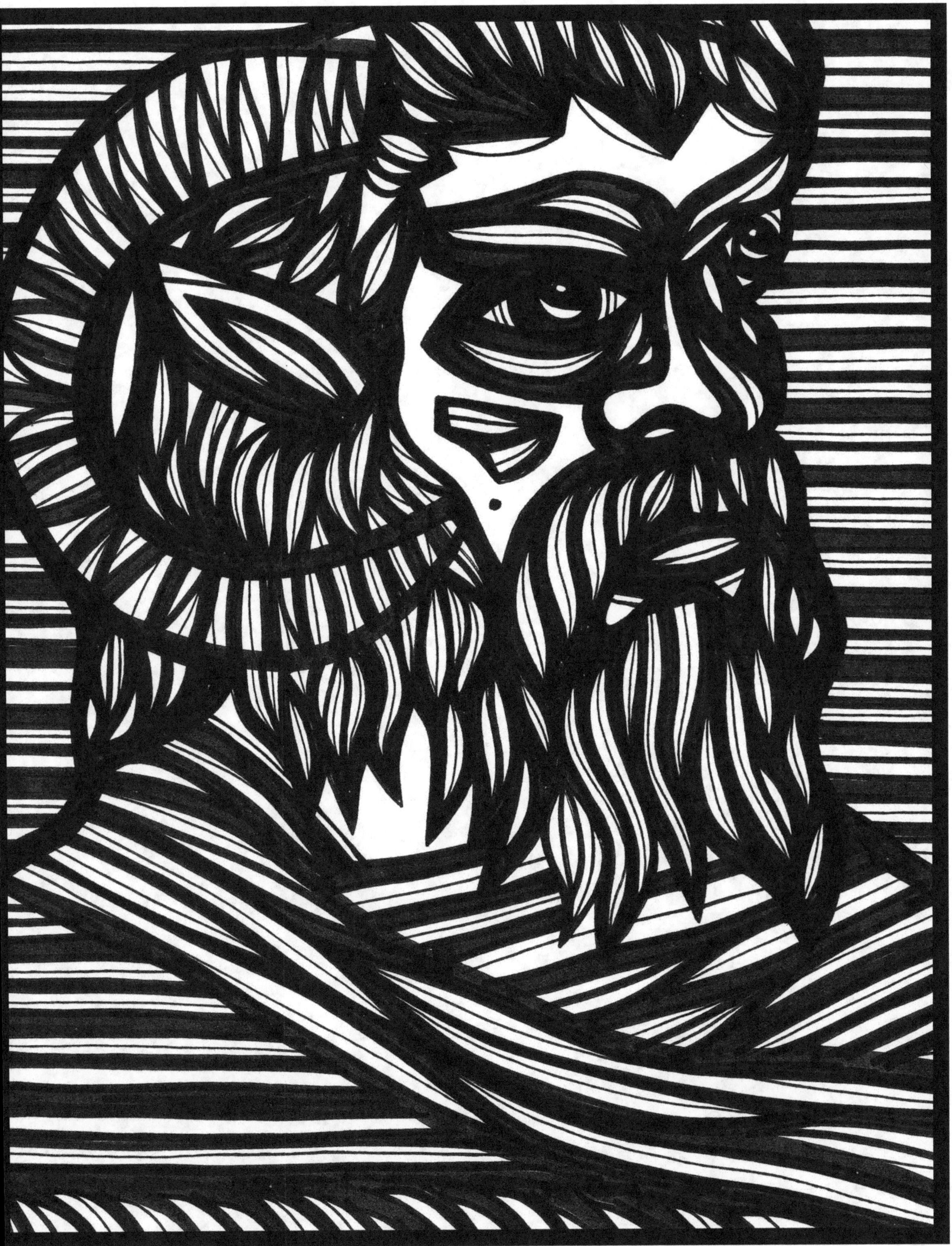

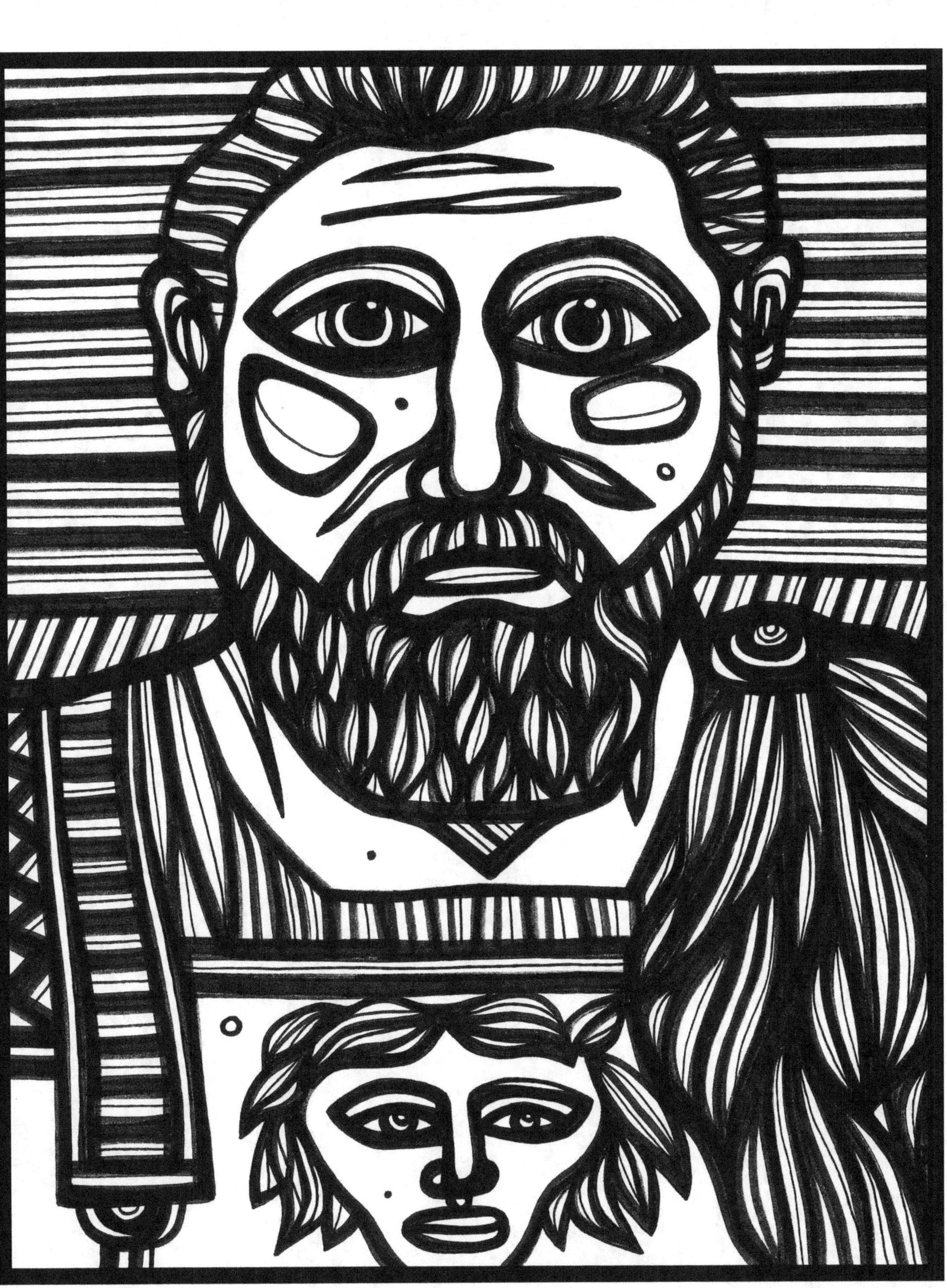

THE END, THANK YOU.

MORE BOOKS: 631ART.COM

www.ingramcontent.com/pod-product-compliance
Lightning Source LLC
Chambersburg PA
CBHW080607240526
45468CB00030B/2461
* 9 7 8 1 7 9 5 7 3 7 4 2 5 *